Entry Level Management
Training Program
Trainer Manual

Management and Beginning Leadership

Dr. PJ Davis

PJ Davis & Associates

Edited by Dr. Sharon Herpin

Revised July 2024

Copyright © 2023 Patricia J Davis.
All rights reserved.
Registration No. TXu 2-352-461
Patricia J. Davis, Volcano, CA, United States
Entry Level Management: Management and Beginning Leadership Trainer Manual
ELMtraining@yahoo.com
ISBN: 9798872297048

FOREWORD

Roll with it.

In my early days as an emerging leader at a large nonprofit agency, I was tasked with overseeing employees, solving crises, and developing programs. What I could have used was a guide, something to help me develop my skills and give me the confidence to power through the challenges I faced daily, reducing the trial and error along the way.

In this training manual, Dr. Davis provides introspective learning experiences for the everyday employee to the emerging leader. Reading through the training manual, you will gain a range of skills from communication to budgeting, which adds to your professional value in the workplace.

Now, you don't just have to "roll with it." With the guidance of this Entry Level Management resource, others will have a roadmap for success. The training provides strategies for individuals to grow their careers, organizations to conduct soft-skills, and invest in the future.

Over the last decade, I have known Dr. Davis as a consultant. She is a champion for the underserved community and uplifts those around her. Dr. Davis is a compassionate and effective trainer. Her passion for people and training is evident in this manual, which took over eight years to publish. I am excited to see the impact it will have on future generations.

This is a go-to resource for emerging leaders!

Michelle L. Tutunjian
Chief Operating Officer
Fresno EOC

About the Author

My story is the same as many leaders, especially in the nonprofit world. The same story can also be found in many for profit fields.

I started in the nonprofit world November 9, 1990, at a wonderful local nonprofit known as Dixon Family Services (DFS), in Dixon, CA. This nonprofit continues to do great work as of this printing in 2024. I owe a lot to them as that was where I cut my teeth on nonprofit management.

I started as a part-time bookkeeper, then became the office manager, and because I outlasted everyone else, I became the Executive Director. I had no management or leadership training and was expected to run the agency. Fortunately, I had a business background that came in handy. But there were no guidebooks or helpful tips on how to be a manager or leader. I had been a leader in the banking industry and was manager of my own branch until I moved into the nonprofit world where I found my passion.

I obtained my bachelor's degree in 2008, my master's degree in 2010 and became Dr. PJ Davis in 2018 at the age of 71. My motto is you are never too old to learn.

I hope this prompts people who may have thought they would never be in a management or leadership position to gain some confidence in themselves and see their world open to new opportunities.

ENTRY LEVEL MANAGEMENT TRAINER MANUAL

CONTENTS

Trainer Introduction 1

Section One: The Basics 9

Section Two: Communication 29

Section Three: Documentation, Record Keeping, and Budgets 53

Section Four: Ethics 69

Section Five: Appreciative Inquiry 83

Section Six: How to be a Leader 95

Closing Notes 117

References 128

With the purchase of this *Trainer Manual*, you can access additional trainer tips through the website, elmtrainers.com. The website also includes helpful short videos for each section of the manual, a PowerPoint slide deck that can be tailored as needed, and a Certificate in Entry Level Management you can download and customize for training participants. Additionally, you are given permission to determine your own fee for the training.

TRAINER INTRODUCTION

Trainer

This *Trainer Manual* is designed to help trainers as they facilitate the *Entry Level Management* training program. It works in conjunction with the *Entry Level Management Participant Manual*. This manual offers additional instructions, transitions, and guidance specific to trainers. Content that is identical to that in the *Participant Manual* is shown in black font whereas text specific to trainers is presented in grey or red.

This program is designed to be facilitated by someone familiar with management and leadership concepts related to being in charge of a team and working with subordinates. As the trainer, you should take time to get to know the participants and ask them to introduce themselves. Ask their names, and if they are working, what position they hold. If they are not currently working, then ask about what jobs they have held in the past or are looking to obtain.

It is important to get a sense of the participants' level of comfort with the idea of leadership. Do your best to put participants at ease and let them know this program is designed to strengthen their assets and provide new tools and skills to help them move into a management or leadership field.

The program is designed to include some lectures, participant engagement in self-assessments, and role play in small and large groups. Resources to support facilitation of the training are also available at [elmtrainers.com.](elmtrainers.com)

Basics of the Training Program

The materials in this training program are provided to you as **information only** and are not part of a professionally sanctioned training course. It is not intended to be legal advice and may not reflect the most current state of the law, forms, or developments.

This information must not be taken as fulfilling professional education/training requirements for certification in any field of management; however, it may qualify for continuing educational units (CEUs). The curriculum is based on principles and standards of common sense and basic management/leadership understanding. This training is designed to be provided in sections. At the end of this training, successful graduates will receive a Certificate in Entry Level Management.

It is important to remember this curriculum is designed as a guide to promote entry level management skills and is not intended to offer any legal advice, nor provide instruction in local, state, or federal rules and regulations.

How The Training Works

The training is divided into six sections. The total number of hours required for completion of this training series should be *no less than six hours* and the training may be presented in a single day or conducted through separate presentations of one or more sections.

Your Role as the Trainer

This training series is designed to utilize one or more trainers to present the material either in-person or virtually. The curriculum was developed to provide a basic understanding of what it means to be an entry level manager. As such, the trainer should be familiar and comfortable with basic management and leadership skills and tools to draw upon during the training sessions to use as examples and enhance the delivery of the material.

There are several leadership styles and many learning methods. It is important for the trainer to be comfortable integrating adult learning needs, remaining neutral, being a positive role model, and using a variety of training techniques that include various presentation styles.

Some trainers use flip charts, presentation technology, role playing, individual exercises, and group exercises. There are several recommendations throughout this training series for both individual and group activities. The trainer may utilize additional techniques to present the curriculum as long as it does not disrupt the integrity of the material being presented.

There are many books on adult learning styles. It is important to address the needs of auditory, visual, participatory, and self-taught learners. Some participants may want to read ahead and work at their own pace. This can be accommodated as long as the participant fully engages in discussion and activities.

Measurable Outcomes

- A pre-post assessment is provided as part of the course. The pre-post assessment measures comfort with and understanding of entry level management and leadership concepts. To gain a baseline measure, participants should complete the assessment prior to any instruction, after introducing the course (the participant introduction is covered on pages 5-6 of this manual, and the pre-test assessment is introduced on page 7). Upon completion of the training, the assessment should be retaken to measure increases based on the training.

- Trainer observations may be conducted before, during, and after completion of the six sections of the training, allowing participants to demonstrate evidence of growth as they progress through the training.

- Additional questionnaires and quizzes are offered as opportunities throughout the training to test self-awareness.

Process for Training

When there are no instructions for a section, the trainer should review the content – not read it word-for-word, but read some key sections and paraphrase other sections.

The wording should be the same in the *Participant Manual* so highlight what you feel is important. There is guidance for specific activities throughout the *Trainer Manual*.

The intended audience consists of two populations: (1) staff wanting to move into supervisory or management positions, and (2) clients wanting to improve employment opportunities to include supervisory or management positions.

PARTICIPANT LEARNING OBJECTIVES

(Direct participants to page 1 in their manual)

Basics of the Training Program: At the end of the six sections, participants will:

- Be able to demonstrate increased knowledge of common terms, definitions, and activities used in the management field
- Understand basic management skills as evidenced by their increased score from pre- to post-test
- Gain confidence in the area of management
- Demonstrate improved communication skills as they relate to entry level management, evidenced by role-playing situations and directly following each session
- Build confidence in teambuilding, as evidenced by instructor observation during and at completion of the series
- Understand quality customer service
- Understand and accept appropriate ethics of entry level management
- Be able to facilitate appreciative inquiry methods of planning
- Be considered for entry level management positions for employment

TRAINER: Review the Overview prior to introducing Section One (Direct participants to page 2)

OVERVIEW

SECTION ONE: The Basics
Covers basic definitions and an overview of several important skills expected of an entry level manager.

SECTION TWO: Communication
Covers basic forms and styles of effective communication.

SECTION THREE: Documentation, Record Keeping, and Budgets
Covers client records, operational records, fiscal records, historical records, and facility records.

SECTION FOUR: Ethics
Covers ethics in general and more specifically the ethics related to entry level management, including confidentiality.

SECTION FIVE: Appreciative Inquiry
Covers uses of appreciative inquiry for staff motivation, board development, and strategic planning.

SECTION SIX: How to be a Leader
Covers basic skills of beginning to manage or supervise others, including building skills and techniques to be a good first-time leader.

TRAINER: Administer the pre-test now.

Direct participants to page 3 in their manual and give them a few minutes to complete the pre-test.

(See pre- and post-test at the end of this manual.)

ENTRY LEVEL MANAGEMENT

Trainer Manual

SECTION ONE

The Basics

Terms and Definitions

We begin this training discussing some terms and definitions specific to management. These terms and definitions are common to both leadership and management. This is not a comprehensive list, but rather one that begins the understanding of leadership. These specific definitions and terms are relevant to this training.

TRAINER: The *Participant Manual-Revised Edition* includes the definitions. Review each item and have them discuss what they think it means or how it may be applied in their current job. Encourage them to write additional notes in their manual or on some paper. (Direct participants to page 6)

Ability: having the knowledge, skills, experience, training, and understanding necessary to perform a task successfully

Administrative Management: using order and a system of doing things

Appreciative Inquiry: a positive method of planning that focuses on (1) what is working well in the situation, (2) what is the dream situation, and (3) what can be done right now to move toward the dream situation and what can be done long term to make the dream situation a reality

Authority: the rights and power to give instructions and expect others to follow

Coercive Power: gaining compliance based on fear or punishment

Communication: ideas, information, and opinions expressed through spoken or written work, symbols, or actions

Competence: a standard level of accepted behavior to perform a given task

Community: a group of interacting people in a specific area; local community may reflect geographic boundaries whereas social community may reflect specific groups of people working on an issue, including partners and other organizations

Customer: direct or indirect people to whom you provide a good or service, which may include fellow employees, external partners, volunteers, or other organizations

Data: raw facts and figures before they are analyzed and presented as information

Database: a system of storing data in a specific manner to be retrieved in one or more ways

Delegate: giving another person the authority to undertake activities or make decisions

Documentation: paper or electronic evidence that supports your actions and decisions

Ethics: moral principles and values

Feedback: input given to someone regarding a product, a situation, or someone's actions or words

Groupthink: a process in which the thinking of the group overpowers or persuades individuals to dismiss their own thinking for that of the group

Honesty: free from deceit or fraud; includes integrity, trustworthiness, truthfulness, sincerity, and frankness

Human Resource Management: the effective use of human resources

Influence: one person's attempts to modify the behavior of others

Information: knowledge derived from data

Innovation: changes or progressions that help process improvements in function, form, performance, or resources that is new, different, and advantageous

Integrity: being of high moral values, accepting responsibility for one's actions, doing what's right when no one is looking, and walking the talk

Internet: a web of networks linked together by active lines through which data can be carried electronically

Leader: someone who leads others by acting as a motivator, seeing the big picture, understanding how to get the most out of others, building opportunities for improvement, and setting a good example

Manager: someone who gets things done with the aid of others and is responsible for ensuring tasks and duties are performed appropriately; a leader to others who manage the day-to-day operations by delegating when appropriate while maintaining responsibility for outcomes

Marketing: a process that efficiently and effectively identifies, anticipates, and promotes goods or services to potential consumers

Monitoring: a method of observing and evaluating

Motivating: a process that prompts action in oneself or others; self-motivation is an essential part of management

Organized: having things in an orderly, tidy, prioritized, and structured manner in which it is easy to find things

Organizational Chart: documented system of recognizing positions within an organization

Partnering: working together for a common purpose based on a relationship with mutual acceptance

Perception: an active psychological process in which what is observed is organized into meaningful patterns; what appears at first glance is one's perception of the event but may not be the entire story

Peers: people of equal status in an organization

Performance Appraisal: a systematic review of a person's work and achievements over time

Perseverance: the ability to continue in an effort regardless of obstacles; overcoming barriers based on determination to complete the task

Prioritize: the art of moving items to the top of one's to-do list as situations change, such as reacting to an urgent situation

Proactive: anticipating situations or events and acting before they take place, or planning for contingencies should various events occur

Quality: essential characteristics that define excellence or fineness (i.e., high quality versus poor quality)

Respect: being held in high esteem by others and treating others as equals regardless of their role

Responsibility: meeting expectations and obligations others have for you

Self-Confidence: belief in one's judgement, ability, knowledge, and skills to complete a task

Situational Leadership: adjusting one's leadership style and being able to affect others to be more effective depending on the situation

Stakeholders: individuals, groups, or organizations that may be affected by your actions or decisions, such as upper management, peers, co-workers, customers, or vendors

SWOT Analysis: a method of identifying <u>strengths</u> and <u>weaknesses</u> relative to significant <u>opportunities</u> and <u>threats</u> for an organization based on internal and external influences

Team: a number of people with complementary skills committed to a common purpose, performance goal, or approach to which they hold themselves mutually accountable

Time-Management: planning and controlling the amount of time spent on specific tasks; planning, allocating resources, setting goals, organizing, and scheduling

Trustworthy: being reliable and delivering on one's word; someone who can be counted on regardless of the situation or influence

Value: relative worth or importance

Management Skills

Transition: Now that you better understand how some terms fit specifically into management, let's move to identifying some specific management skills. We will begin with skills related to organizational ability (Direct participants to page 12)

Organizational Ability

There is a great book by Andy Bruce and Ken Langdon called *DO IT NOW* that discusses 101 steps to getting and staying organized. We will not cover all of them here, but rather some that are important to our training program.

TRAINER Have participants take turns reading the steps and discuss each step as a group. *__Let each person take a different step, read it aloud, then give their own ideas and input__*. A beginning part of leadership is speaking in front of a group and facilitating meetings. This is a process to help participants engage with each other and learn from each other. Some may have more experience than others and the richness of this process comes from peer sharing. If the discussion does not touch on the trainer points noted below each step, be sure to cover them.

#3: Be a proactive person who initiates actions rather than a reactive person who waits to be prompted

> **TRAINER** Have participants consider situations in which this has happened to them or a situation when they witnessed a leader stepping in and being proactive before things got out of hand.

#5: Sort the important tasks from any unnecessary ones

TRAINER Discuss the importance of being clear about critical tasks – they are ones that have deadlines or involve other people waiting for you to act.

#9: Act now if you already know what needs to be done

TRAINER Review the difference between complicated tasks requiring time and resources compared to uncomplicated tasks that require short term action and are easily completed.

#12: Look at whether you put off difficult tasks

TRAINER Review with the participants their day and consider what things they could have done if they took the time to do them at that moment. Consider cell phone and computer use that is not business centered (e.g., games, personal email).

#16: Keep filing up to date and easily accessible

TRAINER Discuss ending each day with 20 minutes dedicated to filing. The end of the day is not a time to begin a new task, so take advantage of that time to file, clean up the office, and organize the workload.

#22: Be ruthless in taking irrelevant actions off your to-do list

TRAINER Talk about the fact that just because we have always done that task, does not mean others cannot handle it. Learn to delegate. Consider if the action means something to the organization or just something you like to do.

#24: Ensure you are not doing other people's work (no micromanaging)

TRAINER Stress the importance of equipping people with the resources they need to do the work (e.g., training, materials, space), then let them accomplish the task on their own. Answer questions, but do not expect people to operate the same way you do. If the task is efficiently and effectively accomplished, do not worry about how they got there. Everyone works differently so do not do their work for them.

#30: Refer to your to-do list to ensure you are meeting deadlines

TRAINER Discuss the idea of taking time at the end of each day to make a list of things to accomplish tomorrow, then begin each day reviewing the list. Modify the list as things are done or if things come up that take precedence over the list. Then move back to the list and continue. Take the low-hanging fruit off the list first (things that take less than 30 minutes).

#44: Realize it is not a sign of weakness to admit that you do not have an answer

TRAINER Discuss that we only know what we know. If we come up to something we do not have the answer for, ask for help. The best leaders do not know everything, but they do know who to ask.

#48: Ensure you understand the real cause of recurring problems

TRAINER If the same problem occurs more than twice, consider why. What is happening and who is involved? Then begin the task of finding a solution to resolve this problem. Include anyone involved in the problem to help find the solution. Leaders engage their followers to learn problem-solving skills.

#61: Remember that if a decision is not an enduring solution, it can lead to a recurrence of the issue

TRAINER Have participants talk about the idea that if the decision we make to solve a problem works – great! But if that decision does not stop the problem from happening again, they should consider moving to the problem resolution process mentioned above.

#62: Never take for granted another person's willingness to act

TRAINER Review the importance of being clear about tasks and who is responsible. Do not assume people automatically agree on something we take as common sense or normal. We all come with different points of view and ways of responding. Some people jump in and act right away, but others will hold back until asked to step in. Be sure to set clear expectations with timelines.

Leadership Behaviors

Transition: Now we are going to move into another management skill and focus on leadership behaviors. (Direct participants to page 14)

Trainer Have participants take turns reading a section and then facilitate a discussion for each section as to what it means to the participants.

Kouzes and Posner present five aspects of leadership in their book, *The Leadership Challenge*. These five elements are constant companions to the management and leadership building process. No manager or leader should skimp on any one of these aspects.

> Model the Way
> Inspire a Shared Vision
> Challenge the Process
> Enable Others to Act
> Encourage the Heart

Model the Way: Take advantage of practicing what you preach. No one is 100% able to master this technique, but we are all encouraged to try our best. Leaders are followed for many reasons, but one main reason is because they do what they say. If you demand respect from others, you will most likely not get it. However, if you demonstrate respect for others, you may gain their respect.

Inspire a Shared Vision: Unless everyone working on a task is on the same page, you run the risk of people taking off in their own directions. There is a Swahili proverb that roughly translates to, "It's hard to move forward if everyone is rowing their own way." Adversaries come together to defend a common threat. This happens in management and leadership as well. Everyone needs to feel inspired to share the same vision. They may take different roads to get there, but they do so by working together and enhancing each other's work rather than duplicating it.

Challenge the Process: Just because something has always been done that way does not mean there are no other ways; there may even be better ways. Take caution to maintain balance and do not reinvent the wheel, as the term goes. Change is only positive when it actually improves all aspects of the task. This is especially true for new managers/leaders. It is not a wise idea to come in the first week and change everything just because you can. However, over time you will understand how things run and when a good idea comes up, go ahead and challenge the existing process in a positive manner.

Enable Others to Act: "It's faster if I just do it myself." Enabling others to perform tasks builds their capacity and may give you more time to do other tasks. As part of servant leadership, if we can enable others to become leaders, we have done a good job. It is wonderful to watch people pull together, accomplish a task, and then say, "Look at what we did." As the manager/leader, you can sit back and take no credit because, in fact, they did it. The result is that a good manager/leader gives others the skills and training to enable them to act.

Encourage the Heart: We all like to hear when we have done a good job. Even those of us who perform for the sake of self-satisfaction appreciate a kind word now and then. We are quick to judge and give negative feedback, but it takes constant effort on the part of the manager/leader to recognize good work and then praise it. It is especially good when the praise can be done in front of others. It lets everyone know that good work can garner praise. One might ask "Why should I thank someone for doing their job – what they are paid to do?" They get paid for their job, but positive input is appreciated. It is an effective leadership technique to encourage the heart. It encourages people to not just do their job, but to do it well.

Leadership Insights

Transition: Now we are going to talk a bit about leadership insights. (Direct participants to page 17)

Before we can become leaders, we must look at ourselves and how we view management and leadership. It is critical to be honest in the self-evaluations in this training. If we do not clearly identify our strengths and opportunities for improvement, we cannot move forward and learn.

Good leaders will spend the time needed to address and embrace opportunities for improvement. They search for chances to become stronger and more effective in their positions. They listen to others and learn from experiences.

Good leaders are eager to learn from others and often ask questions to help shape and mold their own improvement. When you attend a conference or hear a speaker, listen for the key points. Ask yourself if what they are doing or saying is something that could help you become a better manager. Regardless of the topic, you can learn a lot about someone when they speak in front of a group, especially a large group. Watch supervisors, managers, and other leaders to see what you like about them and what might be improved. What steps would you take to make improvements if you were them? Does anything seem to fit your style of management?

TRAINER Have each person think of something they love to do – a sport or something from church or something with friends or family. Do not give them any time to think about it. Pair them up (if odd number one group can be three). Have them take turns sharing with each other what they like to do. Next, have them share in front of the entire group. This helps to get the nerves out of the way when speaking in front of a group, but you may want to set a time limit based on the size of the group.

TRAINER The next segment is a quiz rating participant self-confidence. Tell them to take this quiz seriously as the only person gaining from it is themselves. Give them a few minutes to complete the questionnaire.

Transition: Another leadership insight is self-confidence. As we start this section, there is a short quiz to help you rate your self-confidence. Be honest with yourself as you go through the questions as no one else will see your responses. (Direct participants to page 18)

Rate Your Self-Confidence

This questionnaire is designed to assess your level of self-confidence as reflected in your beliefs about your ability to accomplish a desired outcome. There are no right or wrong answers. Please indicate your personal feelings about each statement by circling the number that best describes your attitude or feeling, based on the following scale:

1=Strongly Disagree; 2=Disagree; 3=Neither Agree nor Disagree; 4=Agree; 5=Strongly Agree

1. When I make plans, I am certain I can make them work	1 2 3 4 5
2. One of my problems is that I cannot get down to work when I should	1 2 3 4 5
3. If I can't do a job the first time, I keep trying until I can	1 2 3 4 5
4. When I set important goals for myself, I rarely achieve them	1 2 3 4 5
5. I give up on things before completing them	1 2 3 4 5

6. I avoid facing difficulties	1 2 3 4 5
7. If something looks too complicated, I will not even bother to try it	1 2 3 4 5
8. When I have something unpleasant to do, I stick to it until I finish it	1 2 3 4 5
9. When I decide to do something, I go right to work on it	1 2 3 4 5
10. When trying to learn something new, I soon give up if I am not initially successful	1 2 3 4 5
11. When unexpected problems occur, I don't handle them well	1 2 3 4 5
12. I avoid trying to learn new things when they look too difficult for me	1 2 3 4 5
13. Failure just makes me try harder	1 2 3 4 5
14. I feel insecure about my ability to do things	1 2 3 4 5
15. I am a self-reliant person	1 2 3 4 5
16. I give up easily	1 2 3 4 5
17. I do not seem capable of dealing with most problems that come up in life	1 2 3 4 5

From DAFT. *The Leadership Experience, 3E*. © 2005-South-Western, a part of Cengage Learning, Inc. Reproduced with permission. www.cengage.com/permission

Trainer Debrief the questionnaire – ask for volunteers to share their responses. Look for high self-confidence. High answers (4 or 5) for items highlighted in yellow show high confidence (1, 3, 8, 9, 13, 15). Questions not highlighted in yellow (2, 4, 5, 6, 7, 10, 11, 12, 14, 16, 17) are negatively worded so high answers (4 or 5) on these questions would show low levels of confidence. Note that there is no highlighting in the *Participant Manual* so you will need to discuss each question.

Management and Professionalism

Transition: Now that everyone completed the self-confidence quiz, let's move forward to talk about management and professionalism. Be honest with yourself as you go through the questions as no one else will see your responses. (Direct participants to page 20)

The saying goes, "You only get one chance to make a first impression." This is true as a manager. Prospective employers, customers, and other stakeholders decide in the first five minutes whether you are someone they can trust and will consider hiring or working with.

There are factors to consider whether someone will decide to hire you or is willing to work with you. Keep their decision process as positive as possible and do not give them reasons to look elsewhere. The same goes for your office space. An organized office with complete documentation and forms at your fingertips will make a good first impression as well.

TRAINER Have the group discuss each item listed below – with examples. Note the examples under each category only appear in this *Trainer Manual* and participants should write down their examples in their manual.

ACTIVITY

(Direct participants to page 21) Group activity. What does a good manager or leader do in each of these categories?

Organization: Uses folders on computers or binders to organize large sections of documents; has a system of filing that anyone can come in and use; has important forms/documents at their fingertips; has documented how-to information on every responsibility; has a structured sense of office and desk

Leadership Behaviors: Respects others; good listener, tempers delegating with involvement of others in the decision-making process (not that others make decisions but rather they are involved in the process – final decisions are up to leader)

Leadership Insight: Gets to know others; shares a bit about themselves with others; watches for strengths and builds on those strengths; praises in public and handles any negative issues in private

Professionalism: Friendly with all – friends with none

Review of Section One

Transition: This closes out Section One. Before we move to Section Two, take a few minutes to reflect and answer the following questions. (Direct participants to page 23)

1. How does learning definitions for management help you become a better manager?

2. What are three ways you can improve your organizational ability?

3. Which of the five aspects of leadership from Kouzes and Posner will you use in your own management process?

4. Rate Your Self-Confidence – what is your take-away from this activity?

ENTRY LEVEL MANAGEMENT

Trainer Manual

SECTION TWO

Communication

Manager Expectations

Transition: In Section Two, we are going to talk about communication and its importance as a leader. We will start with manager expectations, which includes good communication, listening, customer service; organizational and professional communication; interview skill building; and finally, conflict management. (Direct participants to page 26)

A good manager must be organized and have strong time management skills. They must be able to multi-task in thoughts, actions, and communication. You may have someone walk into your office while the phone is ringing and you are in the middle of responding to an email.

You must be able to determine priorities and be flexible when changes occur. Deadlines are important; however, some priorities are more important than others. A good manager learns the importance level of items and demonstrates the ability to make decisions that move things forward rather than slow the process.

Good Communication

TRAINER (Direct participants to page 27) When dealing with communication, remember there are many forms of communication. The basics of time management, follow-up, clarity, documentation, and communication are all management skills needed for success. Review each item asking people to describe what they think of when you say the word or phrase. Get them to go in-depth with examples they personally did or witnessed. The *Participant Manual* does not have the answers. Give them time to write in their manuals or on paper some of the answers for their own record.

Good communication includes:

- **On time responses** – Responding to phone calls, messages, or emails is critical for managers. Managers are often between executives and staff, and must communicate at multiple levels. Time management includes dealing with issues as they arise and not putting things off. When the phone rings, it is better to answer it and deal with things rather than letting it go to voicemail and returning calls. When returning a call, you may reach them right away or leave a voicemail of your own. This can develop into a lengthy process that eats up valuable time.

- **Follow-up** – Be sure to follow through on all tasks. If you delegate a task, set yourself a timetable to follow-up regularly. Do not assume that because you handed off an item to someone else that the job is done. Your responsibility is to see the task through to successful completion.

- **Documentation** – The importance of good documentation cannot be stressed enough. You should be confident your documentation backs up your actions and decisions. Document the task, who you delegated it to, and the timeframe. Document your follow-up and completion of the task. This can be done with paper or a computer.

- **Clarity** – Some issues require delicate yet clear action. As a manager, you must know how to present information that addresses issues in a way that is respectful of all parties involved. How you communicate is important. There are different ways of saying the same thing and people will react to things in different ways.

Transition: Now that we have set some expectations, let's go deeper into one method of communication and see what you think. (Direct participants to page 26)

TRAINER The difference between the following two statements is important – write the two statements from Ellis (2005) on a flip chart if in-person or in a Word document if virtual and have the group discuss both statements:

- "All team members will work overtime until further notice."

- "Due to the latest information on the market opportunities for this product, it will be necessary for all team members to work overtime for the next 10 days to get the design completed. Thanks for your cooperation."

TRAINER Have the participants work in groups to discuss the activity below. After they have worked for a few minutes, bring them back to the larger group and have them share their thoughts. Also note that these statements are **not** in the *Participant Manual*.

Transition: Some topics require more sensitive forms of communication. As a manager, you may need to address issues that arise with staff. Let's go through some topics that may require more delicate or sensitive conversations and consider how you might deal with these as a manager. (Direct participants to page 28)

ACTIVITY

The items below relate to policies and procedures of good office management. Think about each item and consider how it affects your work performance or management style.

Chewing Gum
Smoking
Dress or Office Attire
Personal Items in the Workspace
Personal Calls during Work Hours
Use of Perfume/Aftershave
Food and Drink in the Workspace

TRAINER Sharing how they personally feel about each item allows people to hear other points of view. It is critical for managers to understand the importance of some of these items to the staff they manage. Keep an open mind to hear other views, but ensure safety and fairness for all in the workplace.

Listening

Transition: Let's move on to tackle another element of communication, listening. (Direct participants to page 29)

Communication includes a variety of components, the most important one being listening.

TRAINER Ask the participants the following questions and get some responses for discussion.

- Do you ever feel people just do not listen to you?
- Are you often misunderstood?
- Do you have difficulty understanding what others are trying to communicate?

> One of the most **sincere** forms of **respect** is *actually listening* to what **another** has to say.
> Bryant H. McGill

TRAINER (Direct participants to page 30) The next segment presents 10 keys to effective listening. Review each of the keys and discuss the qualities of poor and good listeners.

Ten Keys to Effective Listening

KEYS	POOR LISTENERS	GOOD LISTENERS
Listen actively	Is passive, laid back	Asks questions, paraphrases
Find areas of interest	Tunes out dry subjects	Looks for opportunities, new learning
Resist distractions	Is easily distracted	Fights distraction, knows how to concentrate
Capitalize on the fact thought is faster than speech	Tends to daydream with slow speakers	Challenges, anticipates, listens between lines to tone of voice
Be responsive	Is minimally involved	Shows interest, positive feedback (e.g., nods)
Judge content, not delivery	Tunes out if delivery is poor	Judges content, skips over delivery errors
Holds one's fire	Has preconceptions, argues	Does not judge until comprehension is complete
Listen for ideas	Listens for facts	Listens to central themes
Works at listening	No energy output, faked attention	Works hard, exhibits active body state and eye contact
Exercise one's mind	Resists difficult material in favor of light, recreational material	Uses heavier material as exercise for the mind

TRAINER (Direct participants to page 31) Ask participants to close their eyes and think of the last meeting or gathering they attended. Reflect on who was there, what the room looked like, and how people were feeling that day. Then have participants answer each yes/no question on the page. Tell them to mark as truthfully as they can in light of their behavior in that meeting or gathering they attended. The answers to the activity are important going forward.

ACTIVITY

Close your eyes and think of the last meeting or gathering you attended. Reflect on who was there, what the room looked like, and how people were feeling that day. After holding that image in your head, answer the following questions.

1. I frequently attempt to listen to several conversations at the same time	Y	N
2. I like people to give me only the facts - then let me make my own interpretation	Y	N
3. I sometimes pretend to pay attention to people	Y	N
4. I consider myself a good judge of nonverbal communication	Y	N
5. I usually know what another person is going to say before he/she says it	Y	N
6. I usually end conversations that don't interest me by diverting my attention from the speaker	Y	N
7. I frequently nod, frown, or react to let the speaker know how I feel about what they say	Y	N

8. I respond immediately when someone finishes talking	Y	N
9. I evaluate what is being said while it is being said	Y	N
10. I usually formulate a response while the other person is still talking	Y	N
11. The delivery style can distract me from the content	Y	N
12. I usually ask people to clarify what they have said rather than guess at the meaning	Y	N
13. I make a concentrated effort to understand other people's point of view	Y	N
14. I frequently hear what I expect to hear rather than what is actually being said	Y	N
15. Most people feel that I have understood their point of view even when we disagree	Y	N

From DAFT. *The Leadership Experience, 3E*. © 2005-South-Western, a part of Cengage Learning, Inc. Reproduced with permission. www.cengage.com/permission

Scoring and Interpretation: According to communication theory, no is the correct response for items 1, 2, 3, 5, 6, 7, 8, 9, 10, 11, and 14; and yes is the correct response for items 4, 12, 13, and 15.

If you missed only one or two questions, you strongly approve of your own listening habits and are on the right track to becoming an effective listener in your role as manager. If you missed three or four questions, you have uncovered some doubts about your listening effectiveness and your knowledge of how to listen has some gaps. If you missed five or more questions, you probably are not satisfied with the way you listen and your followers and co-workers might not feel you are a good listener either.

Hearing
- Accidental
- Involuntary
- Effortless

Listening
- Focused
- Voluntary
- Intentional

Customer Service

Transition: Communication in management also includes how we treat and talk with customers or clients. This next portion of the training will cover customer service, which is a manager expectation. (Direct participants to page 33)

As a manager, you will meet people for a variety of reasons: potential employers, employees, delivery persons, vendors, and other stakeholders. Your customer service represents the company you work for and should always be positive.

Confidence comes with knowledge and experience. The more you read, understand, and learn from others, the more confident you become in making your own decisions. The more time you spend on the job, the more confident you will become in your management/leadership skills.

One of the best tools to use when managing or providing any kind of customer service is the art of saying no without saying no. In other words, use positive language to tell someone no. In the social service world, it might look like this:

Here is an example of negative and positive ways of saying no:

Negative: We don't offer that here.

Positive: We offer these other services that may benefit you.

(Direct participants to page 34) In application, the conversation may go something like this:

Customer: I need a gas voucher.

Staff: We don't offer gas vouchers.

This is a negative thought process and the only thing the client sees is that your organization cannot help or does not want to help. Now consider:

Customer: I need a gas voucher.

Staff: We can help you identify who offers gas vouchers in our area. While we are at it, we can sit down with you and identify some other services we might be able to provide so that you might not need gas vouchers every month.

In other industries, it might refer to some item or service not available at your place of work.

This is a positive thought process and one that allows the client to make a choice.

> **ACTIVITY**
>
> **TRAINER** (Direct participants to page 35) Have participants write down 2-3 things their clients may need that their organization does not provide. Once they have their items, have participants pair up and one be the customer and the other be the staff member. Let the customer pick from the list and the staff member will respond in a positive manner. Watch and listen to how the participant playing the staff member responds and then assist when needed.
>
> In the space below, take a few moments and jot down 2-3 things your clients may need but that your organization does not provide.

Do not assume others know what you are thinking. Do not rely on *common sense*. That is only as good as the experiences of others.

Transition: Along with written and verbal communication, people also communicate through body language. (Direct participants to page 36)

Body language, appearance, tone of voice, and choice of words are all parts of communication. Writing skills are equally as important as the ability to speak clearly. Good communication builds relationships and helps resolve issues whereas poor communication creates misunderstandings, confusion, and negative experiences.

ACTIVITY
Your Favorite Food and Why

TRAINER (Direct participants to page 35)

Ask for two volunteers. Have the two volunteers watch for those who are animated and really into the activity and for those who are just going along with the activity – or any other body language they see.

Write body language types on slips of paper and hand them out to fellow participants. If virtual, ask each person to pick one of the body language types. Have them break into small groups of 2- 3 people and discuss "What is your favorite food and why?"

Be sure they understand what body language they are to use:

Lazy	Excited
Engaged	Disengaged
Distracted	Listening Well
Angry	Not Listening
Happy	Bored

Other body language you would like to show

After small groups discuss for five minutes, bring them all back together and have the two volunteers report out to the larger group as to what they saw.

Listening = Learning

This technique helps develop skills for communication through body language. If we watch for body language as well as listen to what and how things are communicated, we have a better chance of understanding the intent and content of the communication.

Organizational and Professional Communication

Transition: Moving forward with the concept of communication, we will now talk a bit about organizational and professional communication. (Direct participants to page 37)

This section covers things to consider when communicating within an organization or professionally.

Be clear who is in the room:

- Are they people you know well?
- Is it a staff meeting or are there external people?
- Is it a large group of people you do not know?

People all have different levels of knowledge about topics for discussion. Some topics are generally known whereas others might need to be covered in more detail. The level of knowledge about the topic you want to communicate about is an important consideration. Everyone comes with different life experiences, so you must meet your audience at their level then go from there.

What you bring to the conversation is important. When communicating within an organization or professionally, it is critical you know your own level of understanding of the topic. Good managers are known for saying: "I don't know everything – but I probably know someone who knows about this topic." Managers are not expected to know everything but are expected to seek help from others who have more knowledge. It is not a weakness to ask for help…it is considered a strength.

Aristotle's philosophy on public communications goes something like this: tell them what you are going to tell them, then tell them, then tell them what you told them. This advice demonstrates that repetition is key to effective communication. It is your job as a manager to provide several opportunities for people to hear you.

Transition: Let's do another activity, this one is about communication and public speaking. (Direct participants to page 38)

ACTIVITY
The One Minute Speech

TRAINER Have each person pick a topic they know well. It could be professional or personal. Give them 3 minutes to think about how to present. Have each person take a turn in front of the group and deliver a one-minute speech about the topic, practicing the method of telling them what you are going to talk about, tell them, then tell them what you talked about.

Use the *tell them what you are going to talk about – then tell them – then tell them what you talked about* to give a one-minute speech on a topic of your choosing.

Interview Skill Building

Transition: Another form of communication comes into play when we are at an interview for either a new position in our own organization or applying for a position elsewhere. (Direct participants to page 39)

When applying for a management position, it is important for the organization to be comfortable with your communication skills. Giving information about yourself can seem difficult. For some people, it is easier to talk about others. But here, you must convince the organization you have the skills to be in charge and supervise others.

TRAINER Have the group discuss the following four items in a large group. Be sure everyone gives input. This is the time to see how individuals act in a group setting and show their management skills. Tell them to pretend they are going to an interview for a management position either within their own organization or a new company.

ACTIVITY

Consider these potential interview questions and how you would respond:

Tell me about yourself.
What are your strengths?
What are your weaknesses?
Share an example of your ability to work independently.

Conflict Management

Transition: The final element of communication we are going to cover is related to conflict management. (Direct participants to page 40)

When working with any group, there will be times of conflict. As a manager, it is your responsibility to handle conflict. There are methods you can develop to strengthen your ability to resolve conflict. Consider how you handle conflict in your own life.

As a manager, it is important to listen to everyone and make them feel heard, but the bottom line is the decisions belong to you. How you arrive at those decisions can be dictatorial, judgmental, or inclusive. Consider which style you will use and how others might respond to each style.

Consider how you handle conflict in your family or with friends. Consider how you think conflict should be handled at work. Are the approaches the same? Would you treat co-workers different than family or friends? If so, why?

One key element to diffusing a conflict or combative situation is the following:

> Say: "That's interesting, tell me more."

> Or: "That's interesting, can you give me more information?"

The important thing to remember is that you must really want to know more, otherwise it can be perceived as pretentious or fake. Those two words, "that's interesting," helps the other person feel heard and respected. It shows you appreciate their input and are considering what was said.

Review of Section Two

Transition: We have finished Section Two. Let's review what you have learned and reflect on the following questions. (Direct participants to page 43)

1. What are two of the key elements of good communication?

2. List five characteristics of a good listener.

3. Why is positive customer service important? Describe an example of positive customer service.

ENTRY LEVEL MANAGEMENT

Trainer Manual

SECTION THREE

Documentation

Record Keeping

Budgets

Documentation

Transition: Now that we have covered communication, let's move into documentation, record keeping, and a bit about budgets. Let's begin with documentation and specifically client records. (Direct participants to page 46)

Customer Records

Confidentiality is a key component of a successful manager. Whether it is a nonprofit organization, for-profit business, or public entity, the level of confidentiality should be the same. When a husband walks into a bank and completes a transaction, it is important the staff do not share with him that his wife was in an hour ago. If the husband brings it up, the staff member should not confirm or deny if the wife was in earlier, but indicate that information cannot be disclosed.

This same degree of confidentiality should be practiced by all organizations. Care and concern must be given to protect people, adhere to federal and state privacy regulations, and maintain privacy and confidentiality as it pertains to identifiable information of any kind.

Consider your office or work area. When someone walks into that area, can they see identifiable personal information? Are there files or paperwork with identifiable information lying around? Is there a computer screen showing identifiable information that can be seen by someone walking into your space?

Some methods of protecting identifiable information from being seen involve putting away any paperwork you are not actively working on, turning over papers on your desk or work area, and keeping your computer screen from the view of others who may walk into your space. When you are working on something and someone comes in, be sure to cover the identifiable information – be it paperwork or computer screen. This simple effort will go a long way in protecting identifiable information.

Staff permitted access to customer records pose less of a threat as they often already have access to identifiable information and are bound by the same confidentiality clauses in their employment contracts. As such, be cognizant of who is entering your space, especially when it is a volunteer, another customer, a community member, or anyone not authorized to access customer information.

Additionally, documenting interactions is more important today than ever. If something is not documented, it is as if it never happened. Maintaining appropriate and comprehensive documentation is part of the everyday life of any manager. If you do not like paperwork or computer records, then think twice before becoming a manager or leader. The ability to write clearly and comprehensively is another key to being a good manager. Managers often need to complete reports, update sales or other figures, and must be able to read reports and draw conclusions. In the next activity, we will practice completing an annual report based on customers served.

ACTIVITY

TRAINER (Direct participants to page 48) Have the participants break into pairs (if you have an odd number one group may have three). Each pair should answer the questions below the table. Then bring the full group together for a discussion.

Program Year January 1 – December 31			
Quarter	Clients Served to Date	Clients Pending/ In Process	Clients on Waiting List
Q1: Jan 1 – Mar 31	30	15	10
Q2: Apr 1 – Jun 30	60	45	10
Q3: Jul 1 – Sep 30	90	80	0
Q4: Oct 1 – Dec 31	120	95	12

a. What might you include in an annual report to the board or owner? (outcomes, results, accomplishments)

b. What additional information might you want to present? (funding, expenditures, staffing)

c. What conclusions can you draw from the information? (consider the Q3 increase in clients pending or the Q3 drop in clients on the waitlist)

d. What next steps might an organization take knowing this information? (client outreach in Q3, strategies to move clients from in process to completion)

TRAINER Be sure every person gets a chance to participate. This may seem like a simple task, but it is incredibly frustrating for managers when things are not written or reported appropriately.

Data and Reporting

Transition: Now we are going to move on and talk about some of the data and reporting we might see as a manager. (Direct participants to page 49)

Managers are sometimes asked to develop reports but may not necessarily be asked to review the data or what the reports are providing in terms of information related to a service, program, or other aspect of the organization. Some managers will finish a report, turn it in, and simply say, "Wow, I'm done."

Consider some reports or forms you have seen at your organization. Think about why they were developed? What is the purpose of each document?

TRAINER (Direct participants to page 49 and lead a discussion stemming from the questions in the next paragraph)

Think about a report or form you currently complete. Who do you submit the form to? Who else in the organization sees it? How is the information used? Do other people in the organization complete the same or similar forms? How is the information you provide in that form reported?

A term you will hear as a manager is aggregation. To aggregate the data means bringing the data together to organize and present the information collectively. There are many ways to aggregate data elements, and you may see things like totals or averages. Consider some of the types of data you may see in your organization that might be aggregated – fiscal, program, personnel, or facility data may be aggregated. The following are some terms you should be aware of when reading or completing reports and working with data.

Counts: This refers to the number of some important element. Examples may include how many people took a class, the number of jobs filled, the number of orders closed, or the total number of volunteer hours worked across the organization.

Average: Also known as the mean, the average is a central number or point that is representative of the full data set. It is calculated by adding up all the numbers and dividing the sum by how many numbers are in the list. This is useful for understanding things like the typical number of new clients a month or the typical number of orders processed.

Compare: This refers to looking at the data to determine if there is a relationship or difference between two or more elements of data. For example, managers may want to compare the number of sick days taken from one month to the next or the number of accidents before and after implementing a safety program.

Trends: This refers to looking at data over time to see if there are changes or consistency. This can be useful to determine if things are improving or declining over time, such as whether profits are increasing or decreasing.

ACTIVITY

Trainer – Direct participants to page 117 in the back of their book and locate the data table about poverty, population, and unemployment. If appropriate, break them into small groups to analyze the data and come up with some conclusions.

Go to page 117 in the back of the book and locate the data regarding poverty, population, and unemployment. In groups, discuss the following questions:

For each data type, is it more important to know the counts or averages?
What trends do you notice about the poverty data?
What trends do you notice about the population data?
What trends do you notice about the unemployment data?

Record Keeping

Transition: Often times, the data and reports are only as good as the records and information feeding them. Record keeping is an essential part of good management. (Direct participants to page 50)

Records are maintained for the purposes of documentation, historical reference, operating information, audits, and adherence to policy and procedures. Some records must be maintained for up to seven years, sometimes more. Such documents may include:

- Accounting records
- General ledger reports
- Chart of accounts
- Contracts and agreements
- Budgets
- Profit and loss statements
- Vendor lists
- Employee files

Each organization has their own method of financial accounting and record keeping. You may be required to maintain certain financial records whereas other people (e.g., bookkeepers, accountants) may maintain some records either in hardcopy or electronically.

Like documentation in the previous section, records kept for operational use are important and must be accurate, easy to read, and complete. Some records may be hardcopies such as a physical check book or ledger to balance a bank account. Others may be electronic with everything completed online. In business, it is important to use both electronic records and hardcopy documents when appropriate.

Binders are the easiest method of record keeping for paper documentation. Filing paperwork is as key as proper documentation. Maintaining a good filing system will help you as a manager stay on top of things and be able to access paper documents with ease. If electronic files are maintained be sure they are secure and current.

One simple organizational method of record keeping for paperwork is the *Year in a Box by Month* method. This method uses either a banker's box or a drawer in a filing cabinet. Labels are established for each month, beginning with the first month of the fiscal year. Fiscal years can run along the calendar year going from January to December, but they can also be from July to June, October to September, or some other timeframe. The Bylaws of a nonprofit or the originating paperwork for a business determine the fiscal year. Other industries have their own method of determining the fiscal year. Managers should be aware of the organization's fiscal year and be able to establish a record keeping system based on those dates. Within each month, you may need several folders for different types of records, such as bank statements, deposits, and checks. Once the first month is established, you can replicate that structure for the remaining months in the fiscal year.

For vendors records, you may want to create binders or hanging folders listing the vendors alphabetically and then file all appropriate documents in order based on the dates. For employee records, you may want to keep folders alphabetical and file all appropriate documents in order by date, and you may want to have separate areas for current employees compared to past employees. When keeping electronic records, be sure they are secure, current, backed-up regularly, and follow a consistent naming convention.

A modification of the year-in-a-box method can also be used with electronic folders and files. Create a main folder for each year. Within that folder, you can create subfolders for each month. Files can be stored within the folder based on the appropriate month. Additional folders can be created to store important documents, such as client contact information, inventory lists, and employee records. Just like hardcopy documentation, it is important to maintain confidentiality. Electronic documents should be password protected and access should be limited to only authorized staff. Computers should also be backed up and anti-virus software should be used to protect your data.

Budgets

Transition: In addition to documentation and record keeping, we also want to talk a bit about budgets. (Direct participants to page 55)

Budgets are a useful way for tracking expected income and expenses against actuals and help organizations stay on track financially by spending within their means. Good business practice requires a minimum of basic information to track funds coming in and funds going out. Without this tracking system, businesses would not know how much money they have left, where money is coming from, or how money is being spent.

Think about your ability to understand your personal money in terms of income and how you spend that income. If you personally have a system that helps you track your bank balance efficiently, then you are on the right track.

Consider the income sources a nonprofit organization or a for-profit business might see when they track income. Nonprofits might have income from grants, contracts, fee-for-service work, and donations. For-profit businesses might have income from the sale of goods and/or services. Though these seem like different types of income, they both track the same things: actual money in the bank and revenue to be received in the future.

Consider some expenses or costs a nonprofit organization or a for-profit business might see when they track expenses. Nonprofits might have salaries and benefits, office space rent, equipment, office supplies, and program expenses. For-profit businesses might have similar expenses as well as materials for products.

ACTIVITY

TRAINER (Direct participants to page 56)
Have participants break into small groups to discuss the following questions.

***Participant Manual* Instructions:** Think about your way of tracking personal revenue and expenses. Consider the following:

- Do you track your personal finances electronically and capture nothing on paper?
- How do you know how much money is in your bank account at this very minute?
- Are there any outstanding items expended that may have not appeared in your bank account or upcoming expenses to pay?
- Do you use old school documents such as a checkbook or even a check register?
- Do you get paper statements mailed to you?
- Whether paper or electronic, do you review your statements every month? What do you look for?
- Do you use an app or software program to understand how you are spending your money or to help you budget your expenses?

> Every person is different and depending on their experience and comfort with technology, they may use a combination of some of these methods for tracking their personal finances.
>
> Now consider how this may look for an organization. What might they do differently and why?

TRAINER

There is one example of a simple fund accounting budget in the back of your training manual (direct participants to page 118). Take a moment and think about your own agency's funding sources and expenditure items. In this example, the income matches the expenses, which is a balanced budget. You have a profit when the income is above expenses and a loss when the income is lower than expenses.

A more detailed accounting budget is shown on the next page (direct participants to page 119). Here, you can see different revenue sources along the top. One key point is to use the most restrictive funding source, shown on the left closest to the expenditure column. Restricted funding may be grants or donations that came with a specific purpose and can only be used for that purpose. In this example, less restrictive funding sources move toward the right – with the least restrictive funding sources far right. Nonprofit organizations are likely to have columns for donations and fundraising. These may be estimates based on prior years, but not reaching the estimated amounts can result in a loss. Some organizations will not put funds into these columns until the monies are raised and in the bank, or they will use conservative estimates. Organizations can get into trouble if they budget for $52,000 in donations or fundraising but only raise $10,000.

Having a budget is the first step, but it is also important to monitor income and expenditures against the budget. If income levels are less than projected in the budget, your options may be to find a way to increase the income (e.g., holding an extra fundraiser, offering a promotion to bring in new business) or identify expenditures in the budget that can be dropped or reduced (e.g., identifying less expensive vendors, renegotiating contracts, reducing staff time, ordering fewer supplies).

Depending on the size and type of your business, you may have access to an accountant, bookkeeper, or consultant who can provide monthly or quarterly reports, often referred to as budget to actuals, that show actual income and expenditures compared to the budgeted income and expenditures. These reports can help you stay on track financially so you do not spend more funds than available, which helps the organization remain financially stable and solvent.

Review of Section Three

Transition: That brings us to the end of Section Three. Take a moment to reflect on your learning and answer the following questions. (Direct participants to page 59)

1. Client identity and records should be confidential. What will you do as a manager to make sure workspaces protect confidentiality?

2. What information should be included in a report to a board or owner?

3. Why is it important to have a good record keeping system?

4. What does "budget to actuals" tracking mean?

ENTRY LEVEL MANAGEMENT

Trainer Manual

SECTION FOUR

Ethics

Ethics

Transition: So far, we have covered management terms and definitions, communication, documentation, and record keeping. Now let's venture into another important aspect of management, ethics. (Direct participants to page 62)

Ethics can be derived from a person's values, character, and society in general. A person's values are shaped by their family, environment, and education. To say each person shares the exact same values is hard to measure, even when they are from the same family. Suffice it to say, each person has their own set of values.

Some general values associated with social work can be found in the National Association of Social Workers (NASW) Code of Ethics. These values are valid for social work, and non-social work environments. Throughout this section the term client is used, but can easily be replaced with customer. Below are some areas of discussion regarding ethical values generally accepted in the social work field. They are also considered a commonsense approach to working with others.

Value: Service

Work in the social service field should provide the best experience for the client with the available resources. Social workers strive to set the client at ease and they must work together to identify challenges and find solutions. It is a partnership resulting in all parties being successful. Social workers should not dictate to the client what to do, but rather find out from the client what they need and work together to achieve that outcome.

Value: Respect

It is important to ensure the client feels respected and heard. This goes for working with staff as well. As a manager, it is your responsibility to make sure the staff are treated with respect, they treat each other with respect, and everyone treats the clients with respect. Respect is a two-way street.

Value: Integrity

Social workers are expected to maintain a professional attitude in compliance with the organization's mission and standards. Remaining true to the organization mission is a major part of integrity. Also, remaining true to your own core values when fulfilling the organization mission shows integrity.

Value: Competence

Competence is a key component to providing ethical support to clients. Well-trained and informed staff competent in their work bring value to the client experience. Knowing what to do and how to do it is important and makes your job much easier – knowing who to ask when you have a question is also important to the process.

Transition: Let's do an activity together about these values.

ACTIVITY

TRAINER (Direct participants to page 64-65)
Have participants work independently and reflect on their own experiences. Have them write out answers to the following ethical situations, then have an open discussion with the group.

Service: A client is asking for something your organization does not offer. How do you handle the situation?

Respect: As a manager it is your job to gain the respect of others. What kinds of things might you do to gain that respect?

Integrity: Think about any current or previous job – do your core values match those of the organization? If so, name a few core values you share with the organization. If not, what core values do you find are not working together?

Competency: Do you feel you have enough resources, training, and education to be competent in your current position? If you are not currently working, what would you need to feel competent as a manager?

Transition: Other areas of ethics have to do with personal use of company assets, such as technology, and how managers are perceived by others.

As people become more dependent on electronic communication, it can seem easy to mix business with personal activities without even thinking about it. Sometimes, when people think no one is looking, they may attend to personal matters while on the job. What is the harm in checking personal email or financial information while at work?

There may be shades of gray when conducting personal business during company hours. You cannot foresee an emergency at home, so you may have to take a personal phone call at work occasionally and most bosses will understand those situations. However, clarify the rules on internet and phone use for personal business with management or Human Resources.

There is a saying about being a manager or a leader: Friendly with all – friends with none. This means as a manager, you can be friendly to everyone but there should be no appearance of being close friends with anyone you manage or lead. No weekend activities together, no long lunches together, no appearance someone might consider you favoring one person over another. Be sure work is distributed fairly according to job descriptions and experience and no one receives preferential treatment, assignments, or schedules.

Information is readily available on the Internet about ethics in the workplace. Some examples may help refine your approach to being a manager. Review the following scenarios.

TRAINER Use any or all of the following scenarios for small or large group discussions. After reading the scenario, discuss each of the potential options and allow participants to generate their own responses.

Transition: Let's look at some ethical scenarios and break into groups for this activity. **(Direct participants to page 66)**

SCENARIO 1: My Way or the Highway Attitude

Ayelle has been working at a bank for several years. She and her peer, Sally, worked together for three years, but because of Sally's previous banking experience she was promoted to assistant manager. Sally and the manager do not get along and are often overheard yelling and disagreeing on many issues. Sally has developed a "my way or the highway" attitude and it is causing tension in the bank. Sally is over-demanding and picks on one staff member in particular, Keenan. Keenan has started talking about quitting due to undue stress and maybe even suing the bank for unfair practices and harassment. Ayelle listens to Keenan, but does nothing with the information. Later, she overhears Keenan mentioning his intention to sue the bank to other staff members and she must decide what to do about the situation.

What should Ayelle do?

- Take Sally aside and tell her to stop making comments about Keenan.

- Go to the manager and explain what Sally is saying.

- Go to the manager and explain what Keenan is saying.

- Keep to herself and make no comments to anyone in the organization.

- Go to Human Resources and report Sally's behavior.

- Go to Human Resources and report Keenan's behavior.

SCENARIO 2: The Hidden Gifts

(Direct participants to page 68) Grace works for a large company and oversees office supply procurement for the building. To stay within budget, Grace negotiates with several vendors based on price, quantity, and quality. One day, a vendor called her requesting to send more supplies to her company. She knew the copy paper was running low and that the vendor had reasonable prices and quality, so she agreed and placed an order. Along with the shipment of copy paper, there is a box labeled with her name. When she opened the box, it was a nice set of pens.

The following month, Grace received another call from the vendor seeking approval to ship more supplies. This time, Grace declined the offer, stating supplies were adequate and nothing was needed at the time. The vendor became upset and said without an order, she would be in breach of some agreement, but she was not aware of any agreement. He also mentioned if she allowed the order to be filled, he would send along an even nicer gift for her.

What should Grace do?

- Have the salesperson speak to her supervisor.

- Call the legal department.

- Decline the gift.

- Ask for a copy of the agreement.

- Tell the salesperson to ship the supplies and receive the gift in a few weeks.

SCENARIO 3: Reporting an Accident

(Direct participants to page 69) Carlos works at a large home improvement store and was recently promoted to a management position. As he was working one day, he saw Mike accidentally drop a can of paint as he was rushing to help a customer. The can splattered in front of him as he was walking, causing Mike to slip on the paint and fall to the floor. Carlos rushed over to see if Mike was okay. Mike said his knee and wrist hurt a bit, but he was mostly embarrassed and quickly got up to clean the spill. As Carlos helped Mike mop up the paint, it was clear Mike was in pain. Carlos considered reporting the incident, but he did not want to embarrass Mike nor did he want to jeopardize the bonus they would receive for working safely and without any accidents.

What should Carlos do?

- Talk to a supervisor.

- Send Mike to the doctor to get checked out.

- Send Mike home with pay for the day so he can rest.

- Forget it happened and go on with his work.

- Find the security camera footage of Mike's fall and share it with his coworkers.

SCENARIO 4: Ghosting in the Workplace

(Direct participants to page 70) Marco is an accounting supervisor at a mid-sized technology firm. He recently learned his company is being acquired by a larger firm and because they already have a fully staffed accounting department, he and most of his team will be let go once the acquisition is finalized. Marco sends out about two dozen applications and begins interviewing for several positions. He gets an offer from a company and they agreed to a start date a month out so Marco could finalize tasks at his current job that were needed as part of the acquisition process. During that time, another company reaches out to Marco and makes him an even better offer than the first company, so he accepts the offer and agrees to start the following week, which was when he was supposed to start at the first company that made him an offer. Instead of contacting the first company to inform them he would not be working there, he assumed if he just did not show up the first day, they would figure it out. He also did not answer calls from the company because he was working at his new job.

What would you do if an employee ghosted you?

- Call the police to do a welfare check because maybe something happened.

- Stalk social media to see what the person is doing.

- Call their new company to complain and get them fired.

- Leave bad reviews for the new company for poaching your employee.

- Move on and hire someone new.

- Make new hires sign a contract so you can sue them if they don't show up.

THERE IS NO RIGHT WAY TO DO A WRONG THING.

Review of Section Four

Transition: Section Four is now complete. Let's reflect and answer the following questions to see what you have learned. (Direct participants to page 73)

1. What are some of your own personal values that you want to match the organization?

2. How would you address a staff member being observed using the unethical behavior of personal use of the organization's technology?

3. What does it mean to be friendly with all but friends with none?

4. Give an example of an ethical situation you witnessed. Give an example of an unethical situation you witnessed.

ENTRY LEVEL MANAGEMENT

Trainer Manual

SECTION FIVE

Appreciative Inquiry

Appreciative Inquiry

Transition: In Section Five, we are going to begin talking about strategic planning, and specifically using appreciate inquiry as a different way to think about planning. (Direct participants to page 76)

Strategic planning and planning in general can seem like a daunting task. It usually includes things like a SWOT analysis (strengths, weaknesses, opportunities, and threats). This works well for many situations, but it almost has a negative feel to the process…weaknesses and threats. Though they are important in the planning process, another method of planning is appreciative inquiry. Appreciative inquiry has been around for many years and is nothing new, but many people are unaware of the process and how it lends itself to a positive experience.

Factors involved in the appreciative inquiry method of planning include:

- **Discovery**: What gives life? The best of what is .now

- **Dream**: What might be? Envisioning results/impact

- **Design**: What should be – the ideal? Co-constructing

- **Destiny**: How to empower, learn and improvise? Sustaining

Transition: Let's look at each of these elements of appreciative inquiry and how they can be used in your own career planning. (Direct participants to page 76)

Discovery

The first step in using appreciative inquiry is to find out what is working well right now. Look at the situation, team, or entire organization and focus on what is currently working well. Appreciate the best of something. This can be processed by sharing stories and concentrating on those times when everything was going well. Consider such things as quality, value, vision, effectiveness, and outcomes. Conducting a focus group of staff and leadership will help gain a sense of what is working well. Consider listing topics on flip charts or in shared documents to collect information on what is going well within topics such as:

- Leadership
- Human Resources
- Staff
- Technology
- Equipment/Supplies
- Facility
- Management
- Volunteers
- Funding
- Program

Set aside time at a leadership meeting for members to document what they think is working well on each of the topics flip charts. Have staff do the same with fresh sheets of paper so they are not influenced by the leadership and vice versa. You can do this with volunteers and other stakeholders. Gather the data and bring it together in a chart format to show all stakeholders the results. This can be done electronically with shared documents.

ACTIVITY

TRAINER (Direct participants to page 78) Have each person think quietly for a few minutes and then ask for volunteers.

Think back through your career and locate a moment that was a high point, when you felt most effective and engaged. Describe how you felt, and what made this situation possible.

Dream

Once the initial development of what is working is complete, venture into the Dream stage. This is an important phase and needs to be managed well. Allow people time to dream…give them the same flip chart topics with a summary of the working items listed on them for reference. Step back and take a moment to dream of how it could be if everything fell into place perfectly. What would the future look like if all things were ideal? Appreciate the energy created when dreaming of the ideal future. See if there are some common ideals or dreams people are sharing. These may be broad in scope with little details.

Start a new page for each topic and ask them to dream in each topic, if they had the money, facility, personnel, etc., what would it look like? This process will start to show some common threads for dream ideas. It also moves people out of the daily operations way of thinking and into a forward-looking state of mind. Bring the data together in the same chart as the Discover information.

ACTIVITY

TRAINER (Direct participants to page 79)
Describe your three concrete wishes for the future of your career.

Design

To implement and achieve the Dream phase, first look at the "low hanging fruit." What are some items that can be done right away with little resources and time? Are there action steps that can be taken within the next six months that will begin movement toward the final phase? Celebrating small wins is one way to keep momentum in the change process.

It is important to develop strategies for taking on longer-term changes that require both time and resources. Make a chart of things that need to be accomplished in the first month. Include who is responsible and a timeframe. Next, think through what needs to happen in three months, six months, and one year. Be as specific as possible with responsibilities and timelines. Review the chart monthly with stakeholders to make sure you stay on schedule. During the first six months, make another chart that covers years two and three. Then a final chart that covers years four and five. This begins your strategic planning process and should be included in all of your planning sessions and documents.

ACTIVITY

TRAINER (Direct participants to page 81)
Describe how you stay professionally affirmed, renewed, enthusiastic, and/or inspired regarding your career.

Destiny

Now is when you begin to realize some of the dream coming true. Build on this new reality with continued focus and creativity. Look for opportunities to continue moving forward. This is an ongoing appreciative inquiry prospect and one that will allow for new topics and new dreams.

The final phase is sustainability over the life of the organization. Systems should be put in place to track and evaluate changes moving forward. Completing the charts for years two through five with responsible parties, timelines, and evaluation processes are key to ensuring this planning results in positive change. Keep the charts close by and evaluate progress on a regular basis. Include conversations with the board so they are updated regularly. Staff must take ownership of their part on the implementation process and become cheerleaders for moving forward.

> ### ACTIVITY
> **TRAINER** (Direct participants to page 82)
> Describe how you schedule or set timelines for getting things done in your career and how you track to make sure they get done.

APPRECIATIVE INQUIRY

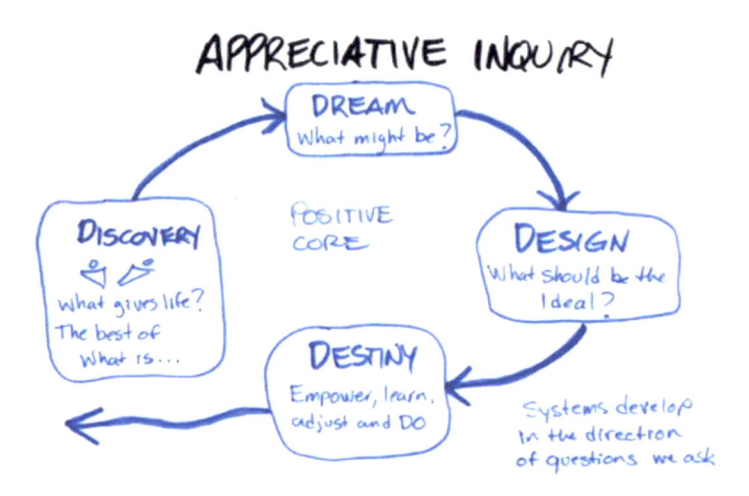

DREAM — What might be?
DISCOVERY — What gives life? The best of what is...
POSITIVE CORE
DESIGN — What should be the Ideal?
DESTINY — Empower, learn, adjust and DO
Systems develop in the direction of questions we ask

Source: Cooperrider et.al

Transition: Now that we have used appreciative inquiry to think about a career path, let's look at some steps of how it can used in your department or organization. (Direct participants to page 83)

Madhuleena Roy Chowdhury in an April 27, 2019, blog post offered some methods for using appreciative inquiry in the workplace:

- Conduct one-on-one interview sessions with co-workers

- Take turns narrating each other's stories

- Ask questions such as: (1) name three things you value most, (2) describe the best experience you have had so far with a client, or (3) what gave you a sense of accomplishment

- Build listening skills by paying attention to each other's stories

- Collaborate in a workshop to build a joint vision for the future

Appreciate Inquiry in Action

(Direct participants to page 84)

Here is one example of how appreciative inquiry was presented to a nonprofit organization working on their strategic planning process. Appreciative inquiry became the main methodology for the entire planning process. Any area of the organization being discussed began with the 4-D's (Discovery, Dream, Design, and Destiny). Focus groups were established and every individual gave input.

Step One: Eight people were designated as the focus group. They were all from different sections of the organization and all had leadership roles.

Step Two: Categories were developed for review – board, facility, technology, communication, and training. A flip chart for Discovery was made for each category with the heading of the category at the top of the page.

Step Three: The leaders went to each flip chart individually and wrote things that were working well in that category. Some people had trouble wording things in a positive manner, but they did move through all categories.

Step Four: The group was brought together to discuss each category to look for themes and similar ideas. After the discussion of what was already in place and working well, the group used the same process for the Dream phase. Then they were brought together again to discuss what was on the flip charts and look for themes.

Step Five: The group began brainstorming the low-hanging fruit items they felt could be completed in a relatively short period of time with limited resources. Then the group developed a longer-range plan for those items that would take more time and many more resources.

Step Six: A plan was put in place for Design strategies and activities to make those longer-range items begin to take shape and move toward completion.

Step Seven: Destiny began to show as some of the items were completed and checked off the list. As they completed items, new ideas sprang forth and were added to the plan. A constant evaluation and planning process was developed.

Review of Section Five

Transition: That's it for Section Five. Let's see what you learned by answering these questions. (Direct participants to page 87)

1. List the components of appreciative inquiry and a brief description for each component.

2. How is appreciative inquiry different from other strategic planning methodologies?

3. How might you use appreciative inquiry in your work or life?

ENTRY LEVEL MANAGEMENT

Trainer Manual

SECTION SIX

How to be a Leader

Leadership

Transition: Section Six is the final section and where we bring much of the material together to talk about how to be a leader. We are going to dive into managing conflict, resiliency, followership, micromanagement, and delegation. (Direct participants to page 90)

Being a manager takes awareness and self-confidence. Self-confidence comes with experience and knowledge in the area addressed. Someone may have a lot of self-confidence in home gardening, but little in the area of agriculture. Confidence may be high for speaking in front of groups of known people, but low in addressing a crowd of 500.

As entry level managers, you may be asked to step outside of your comfort zone and begin the process of becoming a leader. No one can do everything alone. Help from others is needed at some point to get work done. Managers and leaders interact with others daily and need to get the most out of each team member.

Managing Conflict

This is an opportunity to look within yourself and assess your abilities in handling teams and team conflicts. Teamwork is critical to getting things done.

When taking this next self-assessment, you must be honest in your answers. There are no right or wrong answers, only those that reflect you as a manager or leader. The more you understand yourself and your natural tendencies, the easier it will be to determine how to improve your management skills.

These questions are meant to be answered regarding specific team examples. In other words, it is not meant to be answered in how you relate to a family member when a disagreement happens. Rather, think of a time when you were in a team environment and a disagreement happened. Think of how you reacted. It could be a sporting event, a classroom situation, a work-related experience, or anything where you were a part of a team or group. The disagreement may be small or large. It could involve you directly or indirectly. But it must be a reflection of how you reacted or how you think you might react when faced with disagreement in a group atmosphere.

How You Handle Team Conflict

Transition: Let's take another self-assessment about managing conflict. (Direct participants to page 92)

Think of some disagreements you have had with a team member, a student group, manager, friend, or co-worker, then answer the questions below. There are no right or wrong answers. Please circle the number that best describes how frequently you engage in each behavior, based on the following scale:

1=Not at All; 2=Once in a While; 3=Sometimes; 4=Fairly Often; 5=Frequently

1. I shy away from topics that might cause a dispute	1	2	3	4	5
2. I strongly assert my opinion in a disagreement	1	2	3	4	5
3. I suggest solutions that combine other's points of view	1	2	3	4	5
4. I give in a little when other people do the same	1	2	3	4	5
5. I avoid a person who wants to discuss a disagreement	1	2	3	4	5
6. I combine arguments into a new solution from the ideas raised in a dispute	1	2	3	4	5

7. I will split the difference to reach a settlement	1	2	3	4	5
8. I am quick to agree when someone I am arguing with makes a good point	1	2	3	4	5
9. I keep my views to myself rather than argue	1	2	3	4	5
10. I try to include other people's ideas to create a solution they will accept	1	2	3	4	5
11. I offer trade-offs to reach solutions in a disagreement	1	2	3	4	5
12. I try to smooth over disagreements by making them seem less serious	1	2	3	4	5
13. I hold my tongue rather than argue with another	1	2	3	4	5
14. I raise my voice to get other people to accept my position	1	2	3	4	5
15. I stand firm in expressing my viewpoints	1	2	3	4	5

From DAFT. *The Leadership Experience, 3E*. © 2005-South-Western, a part of Cengage Learning, Inc. Reproduced with permission. www.cengage.com/permission

Scoring and Interpretation

TRAINER (Direct participants to page 94) Have each person work on their own and complete the activity. Make sure they understand the scoring process. By comparing scores on the following five scales, they can see their preferred conflict-handling strategy.

Five categories or conflict-handling strategies are measured in the instrument above. To calculate your five scores, add the individual scores for the three items indicated **and divide by three.**

Category	Items	Score
Competing	2, 14, 15	_____
Avoiding	1, 5, 9	_____
Compromising	4, 7, 11	_____
Accommodating	8, 12, 13	_____
Collaborating	3, 6, 10	_____

TRAINER The average score across all 15 items is typically about three. Hold an open discussion asking for volunteers to share their experience and results using the following questions: Which of the five strategies do you use the most? Which strategy do you find the most difficult to use? How would your strategy differ if the other person was a family member rather than a team member? Are there some situations where a strategy in which you are weak might be more effective?

Leadership and You

Transition: We will continue the conversation by talking about leadership and your new responsibilities and new perceptions. (Direct participants to page 95)

When entering a management/leadership role, you must move out of your comfort zone on relationships and responding to others. Entry level management is a step away from the familiarity of non-management positions. Management and leadership require new direction and responsibility unfamiliar to many.

Non-management staff have the luxury of speaking their minds and not worrying too much about how they may be perceived. They can judge others without repercussion. They can have friendships outside of the workplace without fear of compromise at work.

People in management and leadership positions no longer have the luxury of speaking their minds as frequently as non-management. Managers and leaders are held to a higher standard and should hold some degree of distance from non-management as appropriate. This training is intended for entry level management and those with minimal management experience to help determine your readiness for management and to provide tools and skills to help you get ready for a higher-level management position.

If you are a regular staff member, you may feel comfortable speaking your mind to other staff members about issues or complaints regarding the management, facility, operations, or other topics. You may be friends with staff members and engage in social activities outside of work or even do favors for each other.

As a manager, some things may be different. There is an expectation you will treat all staff equally. Fairness to everyone in all dealings is the standard for good management. As stated previously, friendly with all– friends with none. It is important to provide good customer service to everyone and respect each staff member. Things become questionable when you are too friendly with staff or employees.

Remember to exercise good judgement when interacting with staff; it is not against the law to socialize with others outside of work, but the perception could be a sign of favoritism. It becomes an issue if other staff feel left out or feel one or more staff members get special treatment because of their relationship with you. You also need to take caution when posting on social media, as well as when adding or following staff personal pages. Perception is reality!

ACTIVITY

(Direct participants to page 97) You are the manager at a company with about 12 employees. Consider the following scenarios and questions.

1) Co-workers want to meet at a restaurant after work; they like to drink a bit more than you. They also have been known to talk about their adventures at work the next day. Would you join them for drinks?

2) Co-workers have gotten together to celebrate a staff member's birthday. You are invited to attend, sign the card, and pitch in for the gift. What would you do?

Resiliency

Transition: Another aspect of management has to do with resiliency. Let's take another self-assessment to see how resilient you think you are. (Direct participants to page 98)

The following self-assessment is intended to identify your resiliency in business and management. Be thoughtful and truthful when answering the questions as this information is for your benefit. Please circle the number that best describes you based on the following scale:

1=Very Little; 2=Little; 3=Sometimes; 4=Strong; 5=Very Strong

1.	Very resilient. Adapt quickly. Good at bounding back from difficulties	1	2	3	4	5
2.	Optimistic, see difficulties as temporary, expect to overcome them and have things turn out well	1	2	3	4	5
3.	In a crisis, I calm myself and focus on useful actions	1	2	3	4	5
4.	Good at solving problems logically	1	2	3	4	5
5.	Can think up creative solutions to challenges. Trust intuition	1	2	3	4	5
6.	Playful, find the humor, laugh at self, chuckle	1	2	3	4	5
7.	Curious, ask questions, want to know how things work, experiment	1	2	3	4	5

8. Constantly learn from experience and from the experiences of others	1 2 3 4 5
9. Very flexible. Feel comfortable with inner complexity (trusting and cautious, unselfish and selfish, optimistic and pessimistic, etc.)	1 2 3 4 5
10. Anticipate problems to avoid them and expect the unexpected	1 2 3 4 5
11. Able to tolerate ambiguity and uncertainty about situations	1 2 3 4 5
12. Feel self-confident, enjoy healthy self-esteem, and have an attitude of professionalism about work	1 2 3 4 5
13. Good listener. Good empathy skills. "Read" people well. Can adapt to various personality styles. Non-judgmental (even with difficult people).	1 2 3 4 5
14. Able to recover emotionally from losses and setbacks; can express feelings to others, let go of anger, overcome discouragement, and ask for help	1 2 3 4 5
15. Very durable, keep on going during tough times. Independent spirit	1 2 3 4 5
16. Have been made stronger and better by difficult experience	1 2 3 4 5
17. Convert misfortune into good fortune. Discover the unexpected benefit	1 2 3 4 5

From DAFT. *The Leadership Experience, 3E.* © 2005-South-Western, a part of Cengage Learning, Inc. Reproduced with permission. www.cengage.com/permission

Scoring and Interpretation: (Direct participants to page 100)

Add up your scores from the 17 questions: _____

70 or higher: Very resilient
60-70: Better than most
50-60: Slow, but adequate
40-50: You are struggling
40 or under: Consider how you might raise your score in the future

In a world changing faster than ever, one of the most important qualities a person or organization can have is resiliency – the ability to bounce back and thrive in the face of chaos and uncertainty. Some companies offer their employees resiliency training. Resiliency is an important characteristic for managers and leaders in organizations because they must be comfortable with constant questioning and change. You can improve your resiliency by practicing the qualities described in the previous self-assessment.

Followership

Transition: Another element that is often overlooked in leadership and management is followership. (Direct participants to page 101)

Some say a major part of leadership has to do with followership. Followership is being able to follow effectively – and in leadership that means being able to observe your own leadership style and capture what kind of influence you have on others. Being able to see how others are influenced by your leadership can shed light on your effectiveness as a leader.

Someone who discounts the followers' opinions or concerns, is repelled by their input, is not interested in anything other than being a leader – may find themselves with fewer and fewer followers. According to McCallum (2013), there are eight clear qualities of a good follower:

- **Judgement**: They use good judgement when taking direction, including considering what is proper and ethically best

- **Work ethic**: They have a strong work ethic, being diligent and detail oriented

- **Competence**: They must be competent at the task or direction

- **Honesty**: They must be forthright with the leader – especially when things look wrong

- **Courage**: They speak truthfully and are willing to confront the leader if needed

- **Discretion**: They take care when discussing leader concepts

- **Loyalty**: They are loyal to the leader and the organization

- **Ego management**: They check their egos at the door, focusing on the good of all

Being a good leader means having all these same qualities found in followership. The leader practicing an inclusive style will more likely retain followers and have a higher productivity situation than a leader who reaches for autonomy and "being the boss."

Instilling a safe opportunity for followers to share their thoughts and input goes a long way in building strong followership. It also enhances the idea of "many hands make light work." The more input a leader can gather the better the decision-making process.

Followership is an intrinsic part of being a successful leader.

Micromanagement

Transition: Another element of leadership that is important to discuss is micromanagement. (Direct participants to page 103)

Micromanagement is the way some managers hold tight to everything. They may delegate a task to someone but are constantly checking in and making sure the task is done exactly the same way the manager would do it. Micromanagement is one of the main reasons people say they do not like their supervisor or manager. It breeds distrust that can lead to complacency. Staff looking over their shoulders in fear of doing something wrong will be reluctant to give their own point of view. This may keep them from sharing something that could strengthen the result.

Good managers understand the value of their employees and peers. They accept people are different and might approach tasks in ways that may make the manager feel uncomfortable. People can learn the mechanics of doing a job, but it is a good management technique to let them find their own way of approaching the details. Servant leadership (Greenleaf, 2008) speaks to building leadership in others and the importance of leading from a servant position rather than a dictator position.

Example of Not Micromanaging

One example of moving away from micromanagement is seen in the interactions of twin daughters regarding cleaning the fish tank. The mom had her own method of achieving good results: fresh water, clear tank, and happy fish. She showed her girls how she cleaned the fish tank, dealt with the old water, how to handle the fish, and how to clean up when finished. The mom then allowed the girls to help with the process, sharing in which tasks were done. Finally, the day came when the girls could handle this task on their own. Mom had to be physically out of the room when the girls were working…as their way was not her way.

When mom returned, the tank was clean, the fish seemed happy, and everything was dry and back to normal. Their process included laughing a lot, fish sometimes landing in the sink or even on the floor, water everywhere, and some chaos. In reality, they ended up with a pretty good system and accomplished the task in fairly good time.

This example relates directly to micromanaging in business. As a manager, you may have your own way or preference for doing something. However, it is important to provide opportunities for others to accomplish the task their own way, as long as the final result is the same.

Delegating

Transition: The final element we are going to cover is delegating. (Direct participants to page 103)

Delegation gives another person the authority to undertake activities and make decisions. For managers, one of the hardest things when delegating is to actually delegate. As a manager, you are responsible for the result but do not have to micromanage every aspect of the task. Instead, delegate with intent but only after you provide appropriate and sufficient information and training for the person to be successful.

Do not dumb down expectations. Instead, challenge people to live up to higher expectations. When you assume people cannot do a task, you may fall into the thinking of "I can do it faster myself." You must give people the opportunity to grow, value the possibilities in others, and consider they may just surprise you.

One fun way of challenging this process is to delegate the responsibility of writing instructions for making a peanut butter and jelly sandwich. Check for allergies – you can always substitute ingredients.

TRAINER Complete the peanut butter and jelly sandwich activity here. Break the group into two or three teams (depending on numbers). If in-person, provide each team with a flip chart and pens, or if virtual, a Word document can be used. As the trainer, you will need an unopened jar of peanut butter (use another item if anyone has allergies), an unopened jar of jelly, a loaf of bread, a knife, a spoon, a paper plate, and napkins. Ask each team to write down instructions for making a peanut butter and jelly sandwich, telling them it is for a Martian who does not know anything about these items. They must be specific.

Once the teams have completed their instructions, take one of the flip charts and ask a volunteer from another team to sit at the table and follow the instructions. The volunteer can only do exactly what they are instructed to do, no more and no less. For virtual trainings, you as the Trainer should have the items in front of you and do everything just as written by the teams. You will need to reset the supplies (i.e., re-close the jars and bread, clean the spoon and knife) between teams. Alternatively, for in-person trainings you can bring enough supplies for each team.

Complete this activity with each team offering their instructions and a volunteer following the instructions. Debrief after the activity as to the writing of the instructions as well as the perceptions of the volunteer and others observing.

Caution: If the instructions say open the jar of peanut butter but do not say how, it is up to the volunteer (or you virtually) to decide how. If the instructions say with your right hand unscrew the top of the peanut butter, but there is a plastic seal on it, the volunteer has to figure that out. If the instructions do not say to put the lid down on the table, the volunteer must continue to hold on to it during the rest of the instructions.

This activity lends itself to almost all the ideas put forth in the previous material. It includes communication, documentation, a bit of ethics, appreciative inquiry, resiliency, and micromanagement.

Review of Section Six

Transition: We have now completed all the material in the *Entry Level Management Training*. Let's review what was learned from this section. (Direct participants to page 107)

1. What type of conflict manager are you and what can you learn from this?

2. What is delegation?

3. How might you use delegation in your work or life?

CLOSING NOTES

Transition: We have a few closing notes, a capstone assignment, and a post-test to finish things off. (Direct participants to page 109)

One of the points of management and leadership is that it can come at any time in your life and in any given situation. The opportunity to manage something or lead people comes with exposure to different situations demanding action. Sometimes people do not even realize they are becoming leaders or taking on leadership responsibilities. Leadership (and leaders) can change as situations change. A dramatic but realistic example is during a major catastrophe.

Suppose for a moment you are involved in a plane crash. There are some survivors and some deaths. The first leaders begin to act by identifying and caring for injured passengers. The next leaders may appear as the urgent issues have been addressed and passengers are now thinking longer term issues: (1) locating a gathering place a safe distance from the wreckage, (2) enlisting others to help in finding what materials are still available for use, and (3) putting together a plan for survival.

If the event goes on for some time, leaders may emerge as needs change. Leadership may also be distributed as some people will look for available technology or other methods of communication. Other people may be put in charge of locating food and water. Others may begin working to create a makeshift shelter depending on the weather.

Everyone is a born leader in some way. Circumstances may bring out leadership people never knew they had. Generally speaking, management and leadership skills in the everyday world can also be learned, developed, and expanded upon through training and experience. It has been the goal of this training to expose you to some of those skills and build confidence in your ability to manage and lead.

Leadership & Management

Instilling an inspiring vision | Getting important things done | Instilling good operational processes

Capstone Assignment

Transition: It is time for the capstone assignment. Answer the following questions in the space provided. (Direct participants to page 111)

1. Which section was most helpful personally or professionally, and why? How will you apply the information from that section?

2. Which section was the most challenging personally or professionally, and why? How will you apply the information from that section?

3. Name one thing you will implement personally or professionally in the next 30 days.

TRAINER Time now to wrap up the training and facilitate the post-test. Be sure to have participants complete the one-page post-test (Direct participants to page 113). Together, compare their pre- and post-test scores to gauge change.

Using the change in scores, you can track how many participants were able to increase their confidence level.

You may have each participant complete an anonymous evaluation of the training. There is an example of one you can use on page 126 of this manual. Collect all the evaluation forms for review to improve your own training methods. If virtual, you can use Survey Monkey or something similar.

Appendix

United States Population Data

Year	% Poverty	Total Population	Unemployment Rate
2005	13.3	295,500,000	5.5
2006	13.0	298,400,000	4.6
2007	12.8	301,400,000	4.6
2008	13.0	304,100,000	5.8
2009	14.5	306,800,000	9.3
2010	15.8	309,300,000	9.6
2011	16.0	311,600,000	8.9
2012	16.0	313,900,000	8.1
2013	15.8	316,100,000	7.4
2014	15.5	318,400,000	6.2
2015	14.7	320,700,000	5.3
2016	14.0	323,100,000	4.9
2017	13.7	325,100,000	4.4
2018	13.4	326,800,000	3.9
2019	13.3	328,300,000	3.7
2020	12.5	329,500,000	8.1
2021	12.8	332,000,000	5.3

Source: U.S. Census Bureau

Fund Allocation Budget Example

Income		Expenses	
Sales	$90,000	**Admin**	
Events	$10,000	Salaries	$35,000
		Benefits	$ 3,000
		Operations	
		Rent	$11,500
		Utilities	$ 2,000
		Insurance	$ 750
		Equipment/ Supplies	$ 2,000
		Training	$ 2,000
		Programs	
		Salaries	$40,000
		Benefits	$ 3,750
Total	$100,000	Total	$100,000

	CSBG	HUD 1	HUD 2	HUD 3	HUD 4	COVID	GRANT	Donations	IN KIND	
Total Contract	$100,000	$50,000	$40,000	$25,000	$25,000	$20,000	$15,000	$25,000	$10,000	$310,000
SALARIES										
Admin Staff	$ 8,000	$ 2,000	$20,000	$ 3,000	$ 2,000	$ 5,000	$ 5,000	$ 2,000	$ 2,500	$ 49,500
Benefits	$ 650	$ 825	$ 7,000	$ 300	$ 200	$ 500	$ 500	$ 500	$ 250	$ 10,725
Program Staff	$ 55,000	$20,000	$10,000	$ 5,000	$ 1,000	$ 7,000		$ 12,000	$ 5,000	$115,000
Benefits	$ 6,350	$ 2,600	$ 3,000	$ 500	$ 100	$ 700		$ 800	$ 500	$ 14,550
OPERATIONS										
Insurance	$ 1,000			$ 500	$ 1,000	$ 500	$ 5,000			$ 8,000
Rent	$ 5,000			$ 400	$ 1,000	$ 500	$ 4,500	$ 9,500		$ 20,900
Utilities	$ 4,000			$ 300	$ 1,000	$ 500		$ 200		$ 6,000
Supplies	$ 3,000				$ 500	$ 500			$ 1,750	$ 5,750
PROGRAM										
Materials	$ 10,000				$ 200	$ 2,500				$ 12,700
Equipment	$ 2,000	$ 4,575			$ 1,000					$ 7,575
Supplies	$ 5,000				$ 2,000	$ 2,300				$ 9,300
Leasing/Vouchers		$20,000		$15,000	$15,000					$ 50,000
TOTAL OPERATIONS	$100,000	$50,000	$40,000	$25,000	$25,000	$20,000	$15,000	$25,000	$10,000	$310,000

Entry Level Management

Pre-Post Assessment

(For the pre-test, direct participants to page 3)
(For the post-test, direct participants to page 113)

Instructions: These questions are intended to measure progress and growth over time. Answer them honestly as you will be the only one seeing the results. For each item, respond using the following scale:

1 – not at all true, 2 – somewhat true, 3 – absolutely true

	1	2	3
1. I can demonstrate knowledge of common terms and definitions used in the management field	☐	☐	☐
2. I understand basic management skills	☐	☐	☐
3. I have self-confidence in my ability to manage others	☐	☐	☐
4. I feel confident in the different areas of management	☐	☐	☐
5. I have good communication skills relating to management	☐	☐	☐
6. I can build team confidence	☐	☐	☐
7. I understand quality customer service	☐	☐	☐
8. I understand and accept appropriate ethics of management	☐	☐	☐
9. I understand appreciative inquiry	☐	☐	☐
10. I consider myself ready for entry level management	☐	☐	☐

ELM Training Evaluation

1=Very Little; 2=Little; 3=Sometimes; 4=Strong; 5=Very Strong

1. This training helped me become more familiar with the elements of entry level management.	1 2 3 4 5
2. I am more comfortable with the thought of becoming an entry level manager.	1 2 3 4 5
3. The material presented in the training was helpful.	1 2 3 4 5
4. The trainer was knowledgeable about the entry level management materials.	1 2 3 4 5
5. I would recommend the entry level training to others.	1 2 3 4 5

REFERENCES

Bennis, W. (2003). *On becoming a leader.* Basic Books.

Ciulla, J. B. (2003). *The ethics of leadership.* Thomson Wadsworth.

Collins, J. (2001). *Good to great.* HarperCollins Publishers, Inc.

Daft, R. L. (2005). *The leadership experience,* Thomson South.

Dugger, J. (1992). *Learn to listen.* National Press Publications.

Ellis, C. W. (2005). *Management skills for new managers.* Amacon American Management Association.

Greenleaf, R. K. (2008). *The servant as leader.* The Greenleaf Center for Servant Leadership.

Helmering, D. W. (1996). *Being OK just isn't enough.* National Press Publications.

Hoffman, W. M., Frederick, R. E., & Schwartz, M. S. (2001). *Business ethics readings and cases in corporate morality.* McGraw-Hill Companies.